The
Weeping
Rose

A Shakespearean Tale

Thea Barc

ISBN 978-1-64670-303-6 (Paperback)
ISBN 978-1-64670-304-3 (Digital)

Covenant Books, Inc.
11661 Hwy 707
Murrells Inlet, SC 29576
www.covenantbooks.com

To my Heavenly Father, who gave me the ability to put the words together. And to my dad, who always believed in me and shook my hand when I graduated from college. I love you both with all my heart.

Contents

Acknowledgments

My thanks and undying gratitude go to Carlos Byars for his encouragement and technical guidance and to my children for their support and encouragement during the writing process.

A pen-and-ink sketch titled "Dripping Rose," drawn by the talented young artist Athena Colt, inspired the book title, *The Weeping Rose: A Shakespearean Tale*, and is my choice for the cover of the book.

And last but never the least, my thanks to my best friend, Karl, whose loving kindness provided the inspiration for this book.

The poems "Love Letter" and "Tip of the Iceberg" were posted on the Internet at www.poetry.com in 2001. "Tip of the Iceberg" received the Interactive Poetry Silver Medallion award in September of that year.

Prologue

Ever wonder how your life would lie
Could you go back and mend some fences
Undo some bad consequences
What would happen were you to try?

Could you hope to recapture youth?
Fan the spark of old romance?
Give yourself a second chance?
Or gather grains of sagely truth?

Two hearts, who met and felt the same,
But must go their separate ways.
In later years, which seemed like days,
Rekindled their old flame.

Then in true Shakespearean style,
Their friends again drove them apart.
'Tho true love flourished in each heart,
They still succumbed to guile.

Ponder what you might have done,
While our Weeping Rose chronicles the
lesson.

Anticipation

I'm driving east while you are driving west,
About seven-hundred miles apiece before we meet.
At last I reach our designated street,
And freshen up a bit, to look my best.

Anxiously watching for your car
Looking out the window, then pacing again
The clock doesn't move, must be broken.
I'm amazed we both would come so far.

How will we feel after all these years?
What made him get in touch with me?
I've changed so much and wonder, did he?
My mind is racing, chasing all these fears!

Someone comes, and yes! I know that face!
The years meltdown into that first, fond
embrace.

Cloud 9

Our eyes met and twenty years were swept clean
Washed away in a single look
As if the covers of a forgotten book
Clasped the pages of our lives between.

The passion rises and falls, throbbing
Swelling to heights anew
As my body comes close to you
I embrace your heat, sobbing.

Tears of joy wash through me, spilling,
Cleansing all the years of sorrow,
Joy and hope renewed for tomorrow,
Rekindled in a love so fulfilling.

Oh! The promises we made!
Surely, this love cannot fade!

Love Letter

What is love; I hardly know.
I feel all strange inside.
Something is starting to grow.

Could it just be my pride?
I am scared; and yet I'm not.
When you are by my side.

I've loved deeply, been hurt a lot.
I've shared, but Oh! The price,
The past is best forgot.

The lessons were a sacrifice
Tho' hard, I learned them well,
I need not suffer each one twice.

Alas! You've broken through my shell,
For now, my joy is great.
Another lesson? Only time will tell.

Our Strength Is Love

Love is here! Love is strong!
Love teaches us the way to grow,
We need love more than you know,
For life is never very long.

Love is strong. Love is alive!
Guard it well with all your might,
Never let it out of sight.
Insure that Love will survive.

Love is alive. Love is real!
So grasp that feeling, hold on tight.
Love's cure will make all things right!
Love is the thing that makes us feel.

Our love is real. Our love is here!
Our strength comes from love within
Tear down the walls and let it in.
Above all else just be sincere.

The key to life in this great land
Hold on to love and make a stand!

New Love

When I look for a word to describe how I feel,
Serenity comes to my mind.
You are so thoughtful and kind.
Being close to you makes my heart reel!

I am in awe of how someone like you.
Could be in love with someone like me.
Yet I look around and what do I see?
One love that is faithful and true.

We are not together yet never apart,
Our two hearts have become one.
In my world you are the Sun.
And I am the queen of your heart.

One love uninhibited!
Two souls indelibly united.

Tip of the Iceberg

Lying here quietly, watching you sleep
What is the mystery you hold so deep?
I feel you beside me, so warm and so near,
So strong, so sensitive, and oh so sincere.

But I see the sadness, the hurt and despair,
What caused it, I wonder, is there hope of repair?
Somewhere, someone caused you much pain
Making you fearful of trusting again.

One thing for certain, I know and will share,
Everyone needs a friend they can count on to care.
Friends don't come easy they have to be earned,
One of life's lessons, I've already learned.

To have a friend, be a friend, in all that you do,
When you're lonely, remember, I'll be one for you.

Daydreaming

I have walked through the woods on an autumn
    day,
Where the wind blows free, so cool and gay.
Hand in hand with the one I love,
As we watch the fleecy clouds above.

I have seen a stream just after a frost,
When the wind is brisk and the leaves are tossed,
Drifting down on the rippling tide,
While I watch, contented, my love at my side.

My heart leaps out at the sight of a stream,
After a frost, so cool and clean.
Hand in hand with the one I love,
As we watch the fleecy clouds above.

    The Sun bathes all in glorious light!
    And shadows our problems out of sight.

Waiting

Quiet, peaceful, I am serene,
Contrary to the surrounding scene,
Happier than I've ever been,
Since? I can't remember when!

My eyes linger on your car,
Knowing just how near you are,
Already having come so far,
Anxiously watching everywhere.

A dozen people come and go,
Still I wait, but you don't show,
So near, coming, this I know,
Oh, but I do love you so!

At last! I see you at the door,
The longest ever waited for,
I hold my breath a heartbeat more,
'Til I know it's you for sure.

It's you! I breathe! The waiting is done!
And I know that I am with the right one.

Vacation Blues

I wish I could explain to you
Why I'm feeling so left out.
But I really haven't got a clue
What this feeling's all about.

I try to give you room, you see
To do what you must do
And hope that when you think of me
You'll see a love that's true.

I really don't know what to say
To make your pathway clear
But you must travel your own way
To the love you hold so dear.

I wonder if you even know
How hard it is for me
How I long to hold you close
And fear it will never be.

My greatest joy will come the day
That you decide you're going to stay.

A Lover's Song

Staring dreamily into space
Visualizing her lovers face
Isolated in an unfamiliar place
A timid smile sets the pace.

That old dormant aching feeling,
She once was so good at concealing
Never was very appealing
Has returned and set her heart reeling!

The loneliness unknown before
Now comes knocking at her door.
Where once contentment dwelled within
Torment now will not let it in.

A heart so full, no room to beat!
A note can make the day complete!

Surfing

Our love is a sea of passion,
The power deep within,
Each electric kiss a ripple,
Every flaming touch a wave,
Embracing the moments we share.
Fingers touching, skin burning, swells rising,
Each one larger than the one before,
Tidal waves building, cresting, breaking,
Over us as we ride the surf of our love.
The surf breaks over the endless shore.
The ripples gently kiss the beach.
We rest easily in each other's arms.
You gently kiss my hand.

> Our heated embrace ebbs into the sand
> beneath us,
> As the sun is drenched in the cooling water of
> the sea.

Shared Feelings

Lying here on my cloud,
Feeling mellow and proud.
Caught in your sweet embrace,
The vision of love on your face.
I think of the select few,
Who share this point of view.

How I wish there were a way,
That I could show or say,
To the world, "This is real, unique,
Never-ending devotion," but I cannot speak.
For the words don't exist to explain,
This passion that I entertain.

    I bask as the warm feelings grow,
    Savoring this sweet magical glow.

Anxiety

Here I am sitting all alone,
Upon this Valentine's Day,
When you are so far away,
I thank God for my phone.

I miss the little things you do,
The chocolates and treats,
Which make the day so sweet,
All are empty without you.

I sit and stare at these four walls,
And glare at the silent phone,
Too much time spent all alone,
Just waiting for your calls.

Such joy erupts when at last it rings,
Now and forever, my love for you sings.

Dreams

Dreams, failed dreams
Silent cries in the night.
Desperate, so desperate
There is no light.

Trapped, all trapped
No rescue in sight.
Pretense, such pretense
Masking the fright.

Empty, so empty
Robbed of all fight.
Searching and searching
For someone who might.

Love me. Please love me,
Then I'll be all right.

Loneliness Redefined

The sweetest joy I'll ever know
Is being wrapped in your arms.
I never knew that love was so
'Til you captured me with your charms.

Too much time spent all alone
Staring at these four walls.
Glaring at the silent phone
Just waiting for your calls.

Loneliness was just a word
Before you came back in my life.
I thought the meaning was absurd
Until I found you have a wife.

Now the choice is up to me
And I'm afraid of what it will be.

Bittersweet

There is no future, only right now.
No funeral dirge, nor wedding vow,
Just a few stolen moments, no matter how.

We talk of the past, both good and bad.
The strength of our love, the times we've had,
But never the future, for that makes us sad.

Is our love on a downhill slope?
Am I just trying to conjure up hope?
I feel like I've come to the end of my rope.

No graduations, or little league games,
When we talk of happenings, we mention no names.
No, there is no future just impassioned flames.

No family reunions or holiday cheer,
Waiting and wanting are constantly near,
Longing and aching even when you are here.

Love, sweet Love, it's all that we share.
Never enough time to show that we care.
No life together, just love.

...Going nowhere.

It's a Ring Thing

Love is such a beautiful thing
Two hearts, one life to share
As natural as breathing air
Not encompassed by a ring.

My mother always said beware
Of boys whose hands would roam
And never mentioned mom or home
Nor offered to take you there.

It seems like such a tiny thing
Yet boys who are so bold
Still live by those words of old
And never plan to buy a ring.

Loving you, my dearest friend
It is such an awful shame
Knowing I will never share your name
But my heart will someday mend.

You need not say another thing
I know I'll never wear your ring.

Hard Choices

Love cruising down a troubled track
More than a dozen lives derailed
Who knew what carnage was entailed
When we tried to turn time back.

I need to break away from this
This agony is so cruel
The flame grows dim for lack of fuel
Then flares again with a kiss.

Passion and sorrow at war within
My breast, devoid of heart
While yours beats there and we're apart
I am in limbo, unable to begin.

My mind tells me to walk away
My heart cries, "Give him one more day."

Promises Part 1

Remember the heart you entrusted to me?
It aches with longing each time that you leave.
What must I tell it so it will not grieve?
"What fools these mortals be!"

Oh, how I long for the warm days of old,
Those days of promises made by a train,
Joyfully planning when we'd meet again.
Now, your place beside me grows cold.

Betrayed by another we once called a friend,
Foolishly trapped by our own stubborn pride,
We threw our one best chance aside,
Believing our love was at an end.

Searching for love like the one held so dear,
As time after time our relationships fail,
In the light of true love, all the rest seem to pale.
Heartbreak and agony year after year.

I've known life without your passion so deep,
So your heart is safe, this promise I'll keep.

Promises Part 2
Two Hearts Crying

Remember the heart that I gave you to keep?
What must it think when you lie down to sleep,
   ...And the person beside you is asleep?

And what of the heart that you gave me to hold?
It aches with longing for good days of old,
   ...As the place here beside me grows cold.

What of the two hearts entwined in love?
Who thought their union was blessed from above,
   ...And nothing points to resolve?

No one to talk to in the cold lonely night?
No one to comfort me when I wake with fright,
   ...As I lie awake waiting for daylight?

How long must we live with this aching pain?
Is there another chance to become one again,
   ...O God, I must be insane?

Remember how the touch of our hands made us
   melt?
What will bring back the joy we both felt,
   ...And wash away all of our guilt?

Time passes more rapidly day after day.
Nothing is left for either one to say,
   ...And the future just dwindles away.

The War Within

The Good Book warns us not to lead
Another down the twisted path
Or we will face eternal wrath
A warning I'm inclined to heed.

The evil of this world fondly uses
The written Word while you perceive
Wrong as right, yourself deceived
Finding all your rationales are mere excuses.

You cannot choose who falls in love with you
The heart and soul know truth, but flesh is weak
It sees the lies as truth when liars speak
No power on earth can prove the lies untrue.

> Even the Word of God becomes a tool
> When the body chooses to be played the
> fool.

Intercession

The true bard wrote with ink and quill
His tales of heartbreak and deceit
One common theme he would repeat
Wrong choices put everyone in peril.

Actions have consequences all through your life.
All are responsible for things that they do,
When those actions conflict with what is true,
One must accept guilt for the impending strife.

The logical path for one to choose
Should be one that leads to happiness
When each step causes more distress
You've chosen wrong, unwise, you lose.

What must you do to make it right?
Reverse your course and run into the light.

A Walk in the Park

While walking in the park, I see
Birds and squirrels abound.
We share a common ground
Those squirrels, birds, and me.

I sit on the bench, and they flock to me,
Looking for handouts, bread, chips,
Or nuts, whatever from my hand slips,
While I, in awesome wonder, begin to see.

The veil is lifted from my blinded eye,
The creatures vie for every crumb,
So clearly can I see that I am numb.
I know the crumbs are you, the creatures, I.

I hope and dream of what may someday be,
But I see only creatures, crumbs, and me.

Confusion

The time has come for me to grow.
My heart has taken wings.
There are some things you need to know,
For I do think these things.
While I am sure your love is true,
And mine as well is sound,
Your love is divided in two,
And mine has run aground.

My life, suspended, time stands still,
Waiting—from dinner to dinner—
Having a void only you can fill,
Hoping that I'll be the winner.
Promises were made and hearts traded,
We compared Rachel to our plight.
Time spent together, the question evaded,
If asked, we both know what is right.

For whenever we start to plan our life,
You always go home to your wife.

Soul-Searching

My love grows stronger every single day,
Yet I fear my heart will surely break!
Sometimes I think my being here is a mistake,
Though I die inside, I know I should go away.

I ache for you to give me one small sign.
I know your love for me is also strong.
My question is "Just where do I belong?"
Dare I hope someday you truly will be mine?

Time is on the side of those we fear,
As they contrive to wedge us far apart.
Still we keep the song within each heart,
And dream of a day together, bright and clear.

We tackle daily life, as each one must,
And take each moment given on Faith and Trust.

The Agony of Green

Green is a cancer of the heart
It blinds the soul to all that's good
The mind thinks things it never should
Wedging two young hearts apart.

Green slips in by any means
Mostly too much time alone
Wondering why nothing has been done
Dark, lonely nights bring many greens.

Green is the cause of most heartache
Without having a firm commitment
Free thoughts turn into torment
Often more than a heart alone can take.

As yet there is no cure for green
But Faith can wash the true heart clean.

Joy Stealers

Love, real love, is becoming a threat.
One that society holds in disdain.
Where love has no joy, it cannot maintain.
The joy stealers are winning, and yet.

Time is the bond of a love that is true.
It is the target the joy stealers crave.
Need has become the joy stealers' slave.
Togetherness is our passionate glue.

The joy stealers are callous and bold.
They want what they cannot obtain.
They attack over and over again.
Until love becomes tainted and cold.

Love must be kept under lock and key.
For you cannot make love to a memory.

Commitment

Marriage is a sacred state.
Two people become one.
God's work be not undone.
Let all who would abate.

Joy stealers come one and all.
Those who only wish to take.
Try hardest, these bonds to break.
Marriage cannot be allowed to fall.

Promises were made and vows taken.
Long before we met again.
Now our love bears the stain.
Of a marriage vow, forsaken.

The joy stealers are indeed here.
And I have become the thing I most fear.

Choose

Fear, my love, kept us apart.
Fear was there right from the start.
In kids too shy to speak their heart.

Fear, my love, has done us wrong.
Kept us from where we belong.
Though fear has made our love strong.

Fear, my love, has ruled our lives.
Given us mountains of grief, and it strives.
To block us and mock us, wounds deeper than
    knives.

But no more for me, my dear.
We have to see our way clear.
And we have to conquer our fear!

  So choose, lover or wife, be it right or wrong.
  But choose the path that will make you strong.

Futility

Never date a married man,
Though you think your heart will burst.
The time spent alone, waiting for the phone,
Is absolutely the worst!

Never date a married man,
For when he says, "I'll never let you go."
Bet on having every plan,
End with him a "no-show!"

Never date a married man,
Even if he says, "It's all but over."
Just one look from his wife,
And he'll drop you on the next corner.

Never date a married man,
Unless you like chaos and strife.
For when vacation comes along,
Who gets to go? His wife!

Never date a married man,
You'll always be on the outside.
The weddings and reunions he must attend,
You'll wait alone, dying inside.

Never date a married man,
There is too much in his life.
Whenever he must choose, you lose!
He will always choose his wife.

Questing

Where has all the passion gone?
Are we leaving it far behind?
Do we push it out of our mind?
Is that part of our life done?

What waits for us around the turn?
Desire still captures me.
Yet I know not what will be.
Does our passion still burn?

Is it true that love is blind?
Am I your only one?
For me, you are the Sun.
None other shrouds my mind.

    Still, you go home alone each night.
    And I consider flight.

Trying to Say Goodbye

You know how much I love you
I know you love me too.
But do you ever think about
How much I mean to you?

A thousand miles away and more
Yet I still ache for you.
I miss you in my heartfelt core
And now my smiles are few.

Away from you, these empty, lonely years
Trying to go back in time.
I've shed barrels full of tears
Caught up in this paradigm.

Maybe I have finally begun to see
That a future with you will never ever be.

Pining

When you are near, My Love,
    We can beat all the odds!
The future is clear, My Love,
    But then the time comes…
        …To part!

Be of good cheer, My Love,
    Life is what you make it.
If you were here, My Love,
    I still wouldn't have…
        …Your heart!

Happy New Year, My Love,
    I hope you are happy.
Shed no tear, My Love,
    You have what you wanted…
        …A new start!

The Heavy Heart

As you pulled away today
My heart was heavy
For I felt a sense of loss
As if it knew that this may be
The last kiss
Our lips will ever see.

The day broods gloomy as a
Harbinger of ominous events
Coming to taunt us yet again
And my heart grows heavier still
As each passing mile
Widens the chasm between us.

I try to call you back but the gulf is too deep
And I am left alone—my soul to weep.

The Butterfly

The butterfly flits from flower to flower,
Endlessly moving, hour after hour.
Until, at last, it comes to rest,
On that one flower it knows best.
Then the butterfly ceases to be,
What all butterflies need to be—free.
All the dancing on each flower head,
Is over, the butterfly is dead.

I was a butterfly till I met you.
Now, nobody else will do.
Never a soul was as thoughtful and kind.
You, Love, will forever be on my mind.
I know that your feelings are not the same.
I pray that time will extinguish this flame.
My love is freely given without expectation.
You have already shown your appreciation.

Since your happiness is something I hold dear,
I'll love you in silence and not interfere.

Time

I watch the waves erode the sands.
Remembering my time with you,
Wondering, as I often do,
When did we stop holding hands?

Remembering a lone red rose,
Your trademark extra-special touch,
That, to me, meant so very much,
I was glad to be the one you chose.

I miss that hollow of your arm,
The place where I rested my head.
Nothing at all to fear or dread,
And I knew I was safe from all harm.

Love never sees the ravages of time.
A smiling heart is always in its prime.

Flowers

Where have all the flowers gone?
The balloon is shriveled and small.
Sitting here wishing someone would call.
Waiting here once more alone.

The flowers used to bring such joy
And balloons to celebrate
Such warmth they would generate
I feel like last year's Christmas toy.

Now the flowers no longer come
The balloons are all deflated
I cling to the warmth they once created
And the ghost of the lover they were from.

The flowers fade, as do dreams of youth.
Leaving only naked, unvarnished truth.

Broken Hearts

Everything I do, I think of you.
Everywhere I go, I see you there.
I never walk alone, for you go too.
Though you are not here,
    You are always near.

My favorite places are empty now.
I imagine you there, and I know.
You would love them as I do.
Your presence fills the air in a song.
    I miss your touch.

I dream of us going to all the places
That I have yet to see
(Those places meant for two).
I plan how we would spend the time
If you were here and I with you
    And I feel you are near.

The Fitting End

It's been several years since we've re-met.
It was February, do you remember?
Oh, how eagerly I awaited your arrival.
Such anticipation! Such apprehension!
Why did you come? What were you seeking?
Did you find it?
I believed that you had.

Why did you ask me to come home?
Are you so very disappointed?
I thought, *F inally! We can be together.*
Yet the years march on, and we are still apart.
I can't help wondering if I fit into your future.
As well as I fit into your arms.
Do I? Tell me, please, that I do.

We used to fit together so well.
I'll never fit as well with anyone else.

Hope

I await the mailman eagerly.
Your letters bring you near.
Every day without you here
I hold your memory more dearly.

Time has become my enemy now.
I'm caught in a trap of despair.
Knowing that you still care
Wanting to be with you somehow.

I am lost in a sea of sorrow.
My heart yearns for your touch.
The memories of you mean so much
Though hope grows dim for tomorrow.

Yet I believe our love was meant to be
And look forward to the day you come for me.

Drifting Sand

True love knows no one is perfect.
Honor and trust, steadfast and sure,
Joyous and light yet willing to mature,
Each one giving mutual respect.

My heart cries out for someone to love
Someone to have and to hold
Someone courageous and bold
A union to be blessed from above.

The days are longest without you
I see couples everywhere
And marvel at the things they share
Those things we once did too.

Two people walking hand in hand,
While I, alone, am drifting sand.

Surrender

Alone again! Always alone!
I'm so tired, it seems unreal.
I wish that I could always be
The perfect, the ideal.
I wish that I could know the fate
That You have set for me
I wish and wish but still the end
Is harder yet to see.

Always alone! Again alone!
I know our paths must cross
But still, I wish…and wish…
Ever knowing You are Boss.
Dear God, I know that somewhere You
Have yet for me to go.
And I know there's someone new
Yet for me to know!

So I submit to Your divine will
And wait for someone who's out there still.

Moving On

No old shoes and rice for me
I'm as free as I can be
Nobody wants to marry me.

Falling in love for me is wrong
When I love, it's fierce and strong
Yet never lasts for very long.

While I keep searching for *the* one
When all is said and all is done
There always comes the moving on.

Someday I know my search will cease
Someone will come to bring me peace
And offer me that lifetime lease!

Until the day of True Love's dawn
I guess I'll just keep moving on.

One Last Thought

I have always loved you,
I guess I always will.
I often think of you still,
But those thoughts leave me blue.

I miss you very much,
Time continues moving on,
Something wonderful has gone,
I miss your special touch.

Sometimes my thoughts will stray
And I allow my mind to dream
Some future day we become a team
Then I force myself to break away.

Stop dwelling on a misspent past
Close that door and look forward at last.

The Cry

I picked up a book the other day,
And found a rose pressed in between the pages.
The rose must have been in there for ages,
The petals turned to dust, the leaves were gray.

This special rose was given by a lover.
The fragrance sweet, the color once so bright,
Both were symbolic of one glorious night,
A night filled with passion many times over.

That night's passion, like the rose, has faded.
The glorious rose has lost its radiant glow.
As the love it symbolized burned low,
My view of love has now become quite jaded.

> The rosy passion that once burned so deep,
> Leaves bitter ashes, a dead rose, and I to
> weep.

The Weeping Rose

Color fills my eyes with autumn's beauty
Sunshine slices through the morning chill
Warming the ground while all around is still
Dawn comes stealing in to fulfill its duty.

I sit on the veranda, and I dream
Staring at the single rose upon the bush
Past its prime, the petals drop with the wind's
    whoosh
I hear the rose's anguished, silent scream.

The buzz of a sweet honeybee fills the air
It lands on the bush, shaking more petals free
The desperate rose drips beneath the bee
The dewdrops are her poor tears of despair.

My heart feels the rose's tormented pain
And wonders if it will ever love again.

Searching for Answers

How I love to watch a sail
As it billows, full of the wind
The vessel skims across the waves
My troubles fly away on her.

Love has a habit of crashing in upon us
A pounding surf, crashing upon the shore
Then rushing out to sea again
Before we realize it is no more.

It is sometimes difficult to face the inevitable
For it almost always turns out to be
The very thing we dreaded most
Having to make amends for being fallible.

The answers we seek are hard to find
When you refuse to ask the right question.

Life Goes On

It's so sad to see you sitting there moodily,
Dreaming of what might have been,
Thinking about how life was then,
Wishing it could have worked out differently.

But life goes on…
She's gone her merry way.
Though you tried…
You could not make her stay.
And in the end…
She'll have the price to pay.

She's gone away, she's left you—that's a fact,
Thinking about the way you were,
Isn't going to bring back her,
It's time for you to straighten up your act!

'Cause life goes on…
She's moved on down the line.
Through the pain…
You've found a love divine.
And in the end…
She'll have to pay the fine.

It hurts to see the look that's in your eyes,
To know the pain that put it there,
To think she really doesn't care,
I wish that I could make you realize.

That life goes on…
No matter what you do.
Even though…
Right now you're feeling blue.
Someday soon…
Someone will fall in love with you.

At Peace

I hear the peaceful sea sounds
The salt spray fills the air
The eddies of love that we share
Echo in each life it surrounds.

Peace fills my heart once more
As each wave caresses the beach
I feel you, though just out of reach
As I drift aimlessly along the shore.

Peace is mine now that I'm home.
Joy fills my heart once again.
Sunshine helps blot out the pain.
And I settle down, no more to roam.

Peace flows through me like sand.
My passion is subdued. Here I stand!

Tranquility

Sitting on my front porch, pondering
All the things that I should do.
My thoughts, as usual, drift to you
And I cannot keep from wondering.

Are you still with your wife
Because that was "all but over!"
No matter, I've had years to recover
And I am content with my life.

It is peaceful here in my quaint little town.
The zephyr caresses my face.
It doesn't compare to your embrace.
But I have no regrets to live down.

Common sense rules the day.
Serenity is here to stay.

Epilogue

Shakespeare said, "To yourself be true."
Marriage is a sacred bond
It's meant to hold forever
While I am disappointed, I'm not really blue.

The marriage is no longer ignored
Renewed by faith and hope.
If I put a little green in it
Then my faith, too, has been restored.

We marry and faithfulness is just assumed
That love always lasts forever
Then boredom creeps in silently
And loves fuel becomes consumed.

So learn this lesson if you can
And *never* date a married man!

About the Author

Thea Bard is the poetic pen name of author Diane Robbel. Born Diane Hunter in Port Huron, Michigan, she started writing at thirteen. Her first poetry collection was an assigned entry in a literature competition, and she won second prize. This awakened a love for poetry. The sonnets of William Shakespeare were an inspiration to her and, on a lark, she assumed the pen name Thea Bard (The ah... Bard) hoping a little of his genius would rub off on her.

Encouraged by family and friends to pursue a "real job," she obtained an associate's degree in business data processing and began a career that took her to Texas, where she achieved modest success as a systems analyst writing technical documents, user guides, and training manuals to be used by the people at the National Aeronautics and Space Administration (NASA). She continued to write poetry and short stories for personal pleasure during that time. She drifted around the country for several years, doing contract analysis and programming for various companies, eventually retiring to Electra, Texas where she now lives and writes full time.